LOOK!
See Through Katie's Eyes

by

Katie McKay

Copyright © Katie McKay, 2015

Katie McKay has asserted her right under the Copyright, Designs and Patents Act 1988 to be identified as the author of this work.

All rights reserved. No part of this book may be reprinted or reproduced or utilised in electronic, mechanical or other means, now known or hereafter invented, including photocopying and recording, or otherwise without either the prior written permission or the publisher or a licence permitting restricted copying.

Dedicated to Danny,
Steven, Darren, Brendan and Lauren.
My love to you always.

One Life Live It:
Olli,
my beautiful black Labrador.
He came into my life at the right time.

Our eyes blur the truth when we can't bear to see it.
~ Tahereh Mafi

Healing Wishes
Bernice

Love Katie xx

Contents

Preface	1
2011	5
2012	27
2013	35
2014	47
2015	51
Epilogue	73
About the author	77
Katie's music	79
Acknowledgements	81

Preface

It is only the women whose eyes have been washed clear with tears who get the broad vision that makes them little sisters to all the world.
~ Dorothy Dix

I am so thankful to so many who helped me on a journey I had hoped never to take again. My life was normal, until 2011 when something happened to change it.

Cancer.

I have to say that the determination and willpower I have seen in people who live with cancer has made me very humble. My wish now is that the word 'cancer' didn't put so much fear into our lives.

*When life invites you, do you leap,
or do you stay with the safe option?*

The year 2011 was going to be the year I did something I had wanted to do for a very long time: record an EP. So on 30th March 2011, just for fun, I recorded an EP of three songs. I was very nervous about singing for someone else and it took a week afterwards for my shoulders to relax. Although I enjoyed the experience I decided perhaps it was something I couldn't follow through on; the thought of standing in front of anyone to sing petrified me.

I was asked to write something meaningful to me for the inside cover. I went to my little book, *Each Day a New Beginning: Daily Meditations for Women* by Karen Casey,[1] and

---

[1] Karen Casey, *Each Day a New Beginning: Daily Meditations for Women* (Minnesota: Hazelden Foundation, (1981), 2nd ed. 1990). The book gives a message and quotation for each day of the year.

picked a quotation that I felt summed up my feelings at the time. The quotation I picked was for the date 23rd February:

I want to dance always, to be good and not evil, and when it is over not to have the feeling that I might have done better.
~ Ruth St. Denis

Every day that little book helped me through this terrible time, although I didn't realise until later just how meaningful it was for me. On 23rd February 2012, one day after my forty-fifth birthday, I had an appointment in Liverpool to find out if my treatment had worked. It had, and I couldn't believe it, when I looked in my little book for that day's quotation, that the quotation I had chosen a year earlier was the same one I had chosen to put on the inside cover of my EP. This EP was never titled or released; it was just for me, something I needed to do. It wasn't until 2012 that I felt it was the right time to do it for real. I used the three tracks again (after re-recording them), one on each of my three albums, because the words meant so much to me. They were 'Was that my life', 'Because you love me', and 'Wide open spaces'. I now believe – well, I've always believed – that life gives us what we need if we can quiet our minds long enough to listen.

In June 2011, I qualified as a reflexologist and was very much looking forward to treating my family and starting up a business. But I never got to do that.

At the beginning of July I began to have problems with my left eye. At the time I had the decorators in and something just didn't seem right. Colours were not as they seemed. My vision was blurred, as if there was a big greasy fingerprint on my eyeball. I rubbed it a lot and used eye drops, but nothing changed. So I went to my optician who couldn't see anything to be concerned about at first, but asked me to come back if it didn't get any better. A week later I went back to my optician and, after a very scary moment when I thought I was going blind, I was sent to Eye Casualty at The Royal Victoria Hospital where I was initially given the wrong diagnosis.

What I didn't know then was that my life was about to be turned upside down. In October that year I was diagnosed with a tumour in my left eye.

I had no symptoms – no headaches – other than my blurred vision. It turned out that was because there was fluid in my eye. Had it not been there I may not have known I had a tumour until it was too late.

My husband Danny and I live in the Glenravel area of County Antrim, Northern Ireland, and we've been married for twenty-eight years. We have three boys – Steven, Darren and Brendan – and one girl, Lauren, all now adults and off living their own lives. They are our best friends and our greatest achievement.

I know that Danny has struggled with all the tests I've had to undergo. For both of us, this has been the most difficult time of our lives. I can't begin to imagine how Lauren and the boys have coped. I draw great strength from knowing that it's me who is ill and not them.

On one of my visits to Liverpool in 2013 I was asked by a lady how I coped, because her husband was finding it very hard. I told her that since I had been diagnosed I had kept a journal of my experiences as a way of getting it all out of my head and helping me to make sense of what was happening to me. The lady suggested I publish it because it might be of help to others who are travelling the same journey.

So here it is. This book charts my journey through the various tests and procedures. While it's a record of my personal journey, it's also intended to help others who may be travelling in my footsteps.

Hi, my name is Katie and this is my story.

Life can change in the blink of an eye.
~ Alexandra Potter

2011

Monday 26 September 2011

Today I attended the Waveney Hospital in Ballymena for a vision field test. This tests the full horizontal and vertical range of vision to find out what you can see peripherally. Field tests assess your vision for blind spots, which can indicate the presence of eye and brain disorders.

Why is life so tragic; so like a little strip of pavement over an abyss?
~ Virginia Woolf

Monday 10 October 2011

I returned to the Waveney for the results of the previous field test. The ophthalmologist was acting very strangely. Something's not right. He gave me an appointment to attend The Royal Victoria Hospital, Belfast, the next day.

Sometimes it's worse to win a fight than to lose.
~ Billie Holiday

Tuesday 11 October 2011

When I arrived at the Royal the ophthalmologist saw me straight away. It was very different to my first visit in August, when I had waited for two hours only to be told that it didn't warrant an emergency appointment.

The nurse took me upstairs for tests. I had a cannula put into a vein so a dye could be put through it that would show up the back of my eye. I then had scans and photos taken and was sent back to the ophthalmologist, who looked again at my eye and took me for an ultrasound. He told me he wanted to consult with his colleagues and said he'd get back to me. In the meantime did I have any questions, he asked. 'Just please let me know as soon as you can,' I said. He gave me a concerned look and promised he would. I am so thankful to him; although I never saw him again I know he asked about me through my own ophthalmologist.

I went home to wait for the results, not having a clue what might be wrong. I was scared.

A few days later I got a phone call telling me to attend the Mater Eye Clinic on 19th October 2011.

Be still and listen to the stillness within.
~ Darlene Larson Jenks

Wednesday 19 October 2011

My appointment at the Mater was first thing in the morning. First, my eyes were frozen and the eye pressure of both eyes was tested. Then I was given eye drops to dilate my eyes, and given an eye test. After that I was taken to see a consultant who sent me to have a cannula put into my arm. A yellow dye was put through my veins, followed by a green one. The dye was to highlight the veins in my eyes. During this time photographs were taken of the back of my eye.

Later that morning I was taken back to the consultant and Danny was asked to join us. I felt this fear come over me, then I heard the word 'tumour'. Tears filled my eyes. Then I heard 'Liverpool' – I had to go to Liverpool! I could only get treatment at The Royal Liverpool Hospital. So straight away, arrangements were made for me to go. I had been very worried since the appointment at the Waveney, but now I was in shock and very scared.

TUMOUR!

I don't remember much of what was said afterwards.

One of the conclusions I have come to … is the importance of living in the ever-present now.
~ Ruth Casey

Thursday 20 October 2011

There was a package from The Royal Liverpool Hospital in the post for me today. It all hit me: this is really happening to me. I hadn't cried since they told me yesterday, but now the tears came. I cried for the next two days almost non-stop.

I had to be in Liverpool on Monday morning for ten o'clock. There was a form in the package for me to sign giving my consent to donate my eye for research if they had to take it out. I was petrified. Only Danny and I knew about this. I couldn't tell anyone else what was wrong – I didn't want to annoy anyone if they had got it wrong. I didn't want to look stupid – a tumour in my eye? How could that be right? But the package made it all so real – too real. How will I cope? The next three days were a nightmare. In the end I had to tell my family that I was going to Liverpool for tests, but I didn't say anything about the tumour; I couldn't bring myself to say the word.

You don't get to choose how you're going to die, or when.
You can only decide how you're going to live. Now.
~ Joan Baez

Sunday 23 October 2011

Amazingly I got up today and was strong. My arsenicum, a homeopathic treatment to help me with anxiety and fear, was working. The hardest part was leaving the boys and Lauren. I wanted to tell them what was going on, but decided to give them at least one more day when they didn't need to worry about anything.

I got ready for my flight to Liverpool. While I was sitting in the kitchen having a cup of tea a little robin came down and sat on the car. I knew then that I was going to be okay; whatever might happen my guardian angel was watching over me. The robin flew away and we left for the airport to face the unknown.

Words are more powerful than perhaps anyone suspects, and once deeply engraved in a child's mind, they are not easily eradicated.
~ May Sarton

Monday 24 October 2011

I remember sitting in the waiting room of the Ocular clinic at The Royal Liverpool Hospital and seeing a note on the notice board. It told me that one in three people with an appointment at this clinic would have a tumour. I looked around. Everyone was in the same boat as me. Here we were, people from all over the country with our little suitcases, in this one room and we all had something in common – FEAR. I felt horrible. Don't let it be me, I thought, and instantly felt guilty that it had to be any of us.

I had all the usual tests, scans, photos and bloods taken. Then I waited to see the Professor.

The nurse opened the door into a dark world – a night sky – lit up only by a computer screen that displayed a picture of my eye like a huge moon. Danny was asked to come in – I knew straight away it wasn't going to be good news. I was given a tissue and then told yes, I did have a tumour in my left eye. I remember there being a lot of people in the room. The Professor said my tumour was different from ones he had seen before; mine was white, non-pigmented and there was fluid coming from it. He said he thought it might be a seed that had come from somewhere else in my body, suggesting that I might have cancer elsewhere. I couldn't take it all in. Cancer somewhere else! No, I'd know if I had!

The Professor went through the different treatments. There was proton beam therapy, where they put four buttons on positions around the tumour and treat the eye with radiation over five days. Or there was photo dynamic therapy, which is not as successful but can be for small tumours. The Professor opted for proton beam therapy and said he could put me on the list for tomorrow, but first he wanted me to have a biopsy to be sure of what was going on. The problem was that the only person qualified to do the procedure in the UK was in America that week; I would have to come back the following week. So the proton beam therapy was put on hold until I had the biopsy.

I was taken out through another door into a counselling room, where the nurse went through what I had to do next and made sure I understood. I was in shock and cried at the prospect of what was in front of me. I was asked if I wanted to talk to a psychiatrist, but it was all too much for me to take in. I have Danny, I said, and we would get through this together. I was sent for an ECG and bloods to make sure I was ready for the surgical procedure on 1st November, and then we went for tea and a sandwich before going through all the paperwork and catching our flight home. It was a dark and totally miserable night. We couldn't get a flight back to Belfast International Airport, so we had to fly into George Best Airport and get a taxi to Belfast International to get our car and make our way home – home to tell everyone.

How was I going to tell them this – my fragile little mum and my babies. They might be all grown up but I knew it was going to be a big shock for them.

I had planned to go to Cork to see Brendan, my youngest boy, for the jazz festival over Halloween weekend. So we decided to go anyway, but cut it short by a day so we could fly to Liverpool for the biopsy.

I had a great weekend at the jazz festival. It was non-stop music all weekend – it couldn't have been better. No one knew me or what I was going through. I could let the music take over and allow myself to forget for a while. Walking around the shops knowing I wouldn't bump into anyone I knew was also a relief. It really lifted me, and it was great for Brendan to see me and be able to ask questions, even though I didn't have most of the answers.

> *The universal human yearning [is] for something permanent, enduring, without shadow of change.*
> ~ Willa Cather

Friday 11 November 2011

What will today bring! I've been waiting all week for a letter or a phone call. On 1st November I had a biopsy on the tumour in my left eye. It was the scariest day ever. We flew over to Liverpool on Halloween night to be there for an 8 a.m. appointment. I was taken into theatre at 13.10 p.m. and was back out by 13.50 p.m. I had a local anaesthetic at the side of my eye, so I was awake for the procedure.

I lay there frozen with fear in case I moved. I'd been told by the nurse that it was important not to move during the procedure, but to squeeze his hand if I needed to so they could stop. I just lay there wishing it was over, terrified that I would have no control over my other eye, that it might move. 'I don't know why they call this procedure minor – there's nothing minor about this,' I heard the surgeon say before he asked for the forceps. I was thinking, please don't talk – it's my eye you're working on. I could see everything he did. It was a very unusual experience.

As soon as the procedure was over I was taken back to the ward, wrapped in a warm blanket and given a cup of tea and some custard creams. It was over and I sat there, relieved but a little in shock, with a patch over my eye. One hour later I was dressed and in a taxi on my way back to the airport to catch an early evening flight. By nine o'clock I was back home, shattered, with a cup of tea, some shortbread and painkillers, relieved that the day was over, but aware that the waiting was now beginning.

The next day I woke at about six in the morning. My eye was a little sore. I took some painkillers and rested for a few hours. I got up to take the patch off my eye and start my course of eye drops. My eye didn't look too bad and there was no bruising; my face was a little swollen. It was painful putting in the drops. On the day of the procedure itself and while waiting to board the flight home I had a lot of fluid and black tadpole-like floaters in my eye, but this settled down quickly. Yes, it was frightening at the time, but I had been told this could happen so I was prepared for it. It happened again over the next few days. By the third day it wasn't so bad.

I was sleeping well at night, which I was very grateful for in the mornings. During the weeks leading up to my biopsy I had not been sleeping, and almost every night I'd had to get up in the night for a cup of tea to help me sleep. Danny would get up with me and we'd chat, sometimes have a laugh. Now, eleven days on, my eye has almost gone back to normal. It feels bruised. I have a dull pain around my eye and I'm still not able to do very much. If I do it feels a bit strange, like it's coming apart. Looking back on the day of the biopsy, I recall having this very comforting feeling of being held tight, secure, as if I were cocooned. It's hard to explain properly: being so scared took me to a level where I felt guided, looked after and blessed.

I have tried looking at life through one eye. It wouldn't be the worst thing, but I still don't want to have to do it. It frightens me. Will I cope with work? And what about all the stuff that makes me me?

> *Life has to be lived – that's all there is to it.*
> ~ Eleanor Roosevelt

Monday 14 November 2011

The doctor phoned. He asked me to call in for my results and bring my husband with me.

I put the phone down and the fear inside me started to grow. Then the tears fell. I took some arsenicum in water to help me relax, and Lauren made me some tea with sugar. Once I was settled we left for my appointment. In my head I could hear the doctor say, 'It's not what you think.' Was this a good thing?

I wanted to remain positive. The doctor sat us down, then told us that the results from the biopsy had shown cancer cells in the tumour. They had put me on hold in Liverpool suspecting I might have cancer somewhere else. I knew from my first visit to Liverpool that this was a possibility, but I just couldn't believe that I had it anywhere else. My body would have let me know! I had symptoms in my eye; I knew something was wrong there. The doctor explained I needed to have a series of tests and that I had been red-flagged. I was petrified at the prospect of yet more tests and the intensity of the situation I found myself in. I just wanted to go for an appointment and get some good news for a change. Then it was that cup-of-tea moment – when the doctor asked if he could get us a cup of tea – before we were left on our own for a bit. After that we came home, when we had to tell everyone more bad news. Darren came in and caught me unawares. I just burst into tears. He hugged me. I hated this part the most – making others unhappy, and the waiting, of course. My ophthalmologist from the Mater phoned. She had also got my results and wanted to check my eye the next day.

> *Pain is inevitable. Suffering is optional.*
> ~ Kathleen Casey Theisen

Tuesday 15 November 2011

I didn't sleep very well last night – I had to get up a few times and was glad when morning came. We left early to go to Belfast for my appointment with the ophthalmologist at the Mater. I cried most of the way there. I had my hot water bottle with me. It goes with me for comfort when I have appointments, especially in Liverpool when I have to stay over; it helps me get through the night. It's the simple things that matter. I am comforted by the heat against my tummy. This must be so hard for Danny. I have to be okay for everyone, but especially for Danny. He doesn't know what he'll do without me. I know how I would feel if it was the other way around.

The ophthalmologist was great. The tumour hadn't changed shape or size. There was a slight bleed at the back of my eye, but that was normal after a biopsy. She was very positive in the way she talked to me. My bloods had been clear, as was my chest x-ray. She had been in touch with oncology to make appointments for my CT scans – chest, abdominal and pelvis – and my doctor was organising a thyroid ultrasound and breast screening. Hopefully, I'll have these in the next two weeks. She still feels that it's possible the cancer is just in my eye, and she'll be pushing to have the test done as soon as possible. She has been so good and has been a great help to me. I had a more relaxed day today. I told Mum and Brendan, and that has also helped. I've been sleeping better and I cry when I have to. I'm getting better at knowing how to go with what is happening in my body, and eventually I can relax. Sometimes I am stronger than I ever thought I could be.

Zeal is the faculty igniting the other mind powers into the flame of activity.
~ Sylvia Stitt Edwards

Friday 18 November 2011

I've got a date for my CT scans – 5th December. My ophthalmologist thinks this is too long to wait so she's trying to get it brought forward. She feels it needs to be done sooner. My doctor phoned today and wishes things would move quicker. I'm to keep in touch with him daily to let him know how I'm getting on. Although I didn't do it, it was good to know I could. He will keep the pressure on to get me seen quicker. I have got through another week.

Do not compare yourself to others, for you are a unique and wonderful creation. Make your own beautiful footprints in the snow.
~ Barbara Kimball

Saturday 19 November 2011

It's only five weeks to Christmas. I've been helping Steven to make the Christmas cakes and prepare the puddings for stirring. Darren and Dad have the Charolais calf out walking, getting him ready for next year's show, which is nice to see. Lauren is off for a sleepover with her friend. Brendan phoned from Cork for a chat. Life goes on, one day at a time, and there is a little sunshine every day, please God.

Experience is a good teacher, but she sends in terrific bills.
~ Minna Antrim

Monday 21 November 2011

I got a phone call today. I'll be going for my CT scan of chest, abdomen and pelvis on Thursday 24th November.

> ... *as awareness increases, the need for personal secrecy almost proportionately decreases.*
> ~ Charlotte Painter

Thursday 24 November 2011

Had my scans today. Now I have to wait until Tuesday for the results and to have my first appointment with the oncologist. It's scary.

I was back to see my ophthalmologist on Wednesday. I was also seen by another ophthalmologist that I'd first met at The Royal Victoria Eye Clinic. She had referred me to the Mater Eye Clinic because she said I was 'an interesting case'. She was impressed with the biopsy. My eye was still a little bruised but the layers of the eye were intact.

Lauren was very upset tonight – we both were. Woke this morning to a phone call. Danny's uncle John had passed away in the early hours of the morning. I was very upset because I was going to call in to visit him when I was at the hospital for my tests today. I was always very fond of him. On the day of our marriage he wanted to buy me a drink. I said, 'I don't drink, but thanks.' He bought me a coke and said 'I hope there's twins in it.' Nine months later I had a boy. The next time we met he asked how many children I had. I told him we had three boys and went on to tell him the story. He took me to the bar, bought me a coke and said the same words: 'I hope there's twins in it.' Nine months later I got my little girl. It had been four years since I had my boys and I thought I'd had my lot. We love this story and the fact that he was a part of it.

It has been a hard day, and waiting is hard on Lauren. She had a school test today and didn't let on. GCSE year is stressful enough for her without all this going on. Is there ever a good time to be ill?

'If onlys' are lonely.
~ Morgan Jennings

Friday 25 November 2011

I called in with the doctor today. He was still frustrated at not being able to get me an appointment for breast screening. He phoned them again while I was there and amazingly got an appointment. They even gave him the choice of two dates. I'm going on 2nd December at 9 a.m. We had a long chat. He doesn't know how I cope with the waiting.

Change occurs when one becomes what she is, not when she tries to become what she is not.
~ Ruth P. Freedman

Tuesday 29 November 2011

It's my first visit to the oncology department at the City Hospital in Belfast. This afternoon I meet with the oncologist who explained my test results from the scans last Thursday. A few spots showed up on my liver and kidneys, and in the lining of my lungs. I'm to have an ultrasound on my liver and kidneys and possibly a biopsy on my lungs, but they're pretty confident they are going to be okay. She said that these are normal things to see when someone has had a body scan, but because they are investigating a possible primary site somewhere else in my body they have to be sure.

Then I met with another oncologist, who enquired about my tumour and questioned me about family history and lifestyle. He told me how he'd like to proceed: I would have a planning day on 7th December, followed by five days of radiation treatment possibly to both eyes. He hoped to get started before Christmas, which was still two full weeks away. Both oncologists examined me for anything suspicious and found no cause for concern. They were both very nice, and although I left feeling relieved I still face more tests and I'm unsure about the treatment he's suggesting. I need to talk to my ophthalmologist at the Mater to make sure I am getting the best advice.

Faith is like a balloon. If you've got it, you're filled.
If you don't, you're empty.
~ Peggy Cahn

Friday 2 December 2011

Today I went for breast screening at Antrim Area Hospital. The doctor was very interested in me, and wanted to know the whole story and about how the biopsy was done. Then he checked me over, marked a spot with a pen, and sent me for a mammogram and an ultrasound. Thankfully nothing was found, because this was what they call a one-stop shop, I didn't have to wait weeks for the results.

The old woman I shall become will be quite different from the woman I am now.
Another I, is becoming …
~ George Sand

Monday 5 December 2011

I had the thyroid ultrasound at the Causeway Hospital this afternoon. I have to wait eight to ten days for the results, the nurse says. This is the second time I have had to wait for this test result, the difference being that the first time I had to have a biopsy. The first time was almost thirteen years ago. I had taken my daughter to see a specialist. While she was sitting on my knee the doctor noticed a lump on my throat and after a few different appointments I was referred to the hospital; during the appointment a biopsy was taken. I was not prepared for it; having four very young children at home I was very scared. The period of time I had to wait for the results sent me into a bit of a state. The doctor noticed the lump in November 1998, and I had the biopsy January 1999, the night before we took our oldest boy, Steven, then aged eleven, to look around the secondary school he would be attending in September. It was a night we had been excited about, but with the test in my head it was a night of mixed emotions for me. I received a letter in February 1999 to say that they had not got enough in the biopsy to reach a conclusive result, so I was to have it checked regularly by my doctor. I can't believe it was so long ago. I have been much more worried about this test because one lady I spoke to on the day I had the biopsy of my eye told me she had had breast cancer twelve years earlier and her secondary was in her eye. I was very scared that maybe they had missed something in my first thyroid test.

It's a long baptism into the seas of humankind, my daughter. Better immersion than to live untouched.

~ Tillie Olsen

Tuesday 6 December 2011

Tomorrow I am booked in for my planning day. I will have my mask made and be prepared for radiation treatment to start. The mask is made so radiation hits my eye only. I got a phone call from my oncologist's secretary yesterday morning: 'Sorry about the short notice, but they'd like you to come on Wednesday. They have a very busy day but would really like to get you started on your treatment. Could you be here at 8.30 a.m. so he can fit you in first?' I put down the phone, told Danny and then burst into tears! The doctor's urgency scares me a little. For a while I feel shaken up inside; then suddenly it leaves me and I get on with my day as if nothing is wrong. I want someone to slap me and say nothing is wrong, you're okay, but they don't and I carry on waiting for someone to fix me.

I'm worried about the treatment. It's a scary word, 'radiation'. I never thought I'd have to do it. I've hated tablets ever since my days on Seroxate, when I feared everything and everyone. In 1999, I spent seven months on them, and got off them with the help of a herbalist. I would never have been on them if I'd had someone to talk to while I went through the thyroid tests and the biopsy. It was the wait for the test results that was the worst bit, though. My head had conjured up all the worst-case scenarios and my anxiety was made worse by the fact that I had a young family. I know now I just needed to talk it out, but the doctor decided I was depressed and tablets were my only option. I soon discovered the tablets *made* me depressed and I became locked in myself. I worked hard to get off them; it was a very difficult period. I never want to go back there again. I'm scared I might have to take something now and be on it for the rest of my life, harming some other part of me in the process.

I don't know if I could have avoided what's happening to me. I take comfort today in the fact that my other tests have been clear. I've never smoked or drank, and I've always looked after myself healthwise as best I could. Perhaps being healthy, and the fact that I love life, laugh a lot, have a supportive husband and kids (well, most of the time – they do get on my nerves sometimes, and I on theirs, but that's life and we love each other deeply) will be the things that save me.

I had a chat with my ophthalmologist today about my treatment. She will contact the Professor in Liverpool and get back to me. She wants to make sure I get the right treatment and is worried that if I get radiation treatment to the whole eye I might lose my sight or have other complications, never mind the fact that they want to do both eyes. She doesn't want anyone to touch my other eye. The oncologists are scared of a spread. I am praying, please do the right thing. My ophthalmologist thinks that with proton beam therapy there will be less damage to my eyesight. I'll just have to wait and see.

The day took a strange turn. I got a letter telling me to go for an ultrasound of my liver and kidneys on 15th December. I then got a call from my doctor about my thyroid results. They were clear. Then my ophthalmologist phoned to say the Professor wanted me back in Liverpool on 15th December, which meant I had to put my treatment plan at the City Hospital on hold and reschedule the ultrasound scans. The girl I spoke to was really nice and gave me an appointment for the next day (7th December) so that I'd have the results back in time to take to Liverpool. My radiation treatment has now been put on hold.

Then I got a phone call from the Professor's secretary in Liverpool to say that the Professor would be away on the 15th but he wanted to see me, so the date was changed to the 22nd December. A crazy day!

Each day provides its own gifts.
~ Ruth P. Freedman

Sunday 11 December 2011

I went on the 7th for my ultrasound test of my liver and kidneys. The results were clear. It's possible they may want to do an MRI of my breasts and a biopsy of the lining of my lungs where they found some spotting in the CT scan, but I hope I'm done with the tests. Looking back, I'm glad now that they found nothing, but it has been a very scary time for us all. I can't help thinking that the more they look the more likely they are to find something, and I want them to stop in case they do. I just want to get my eye sorted and resume a normal life.

It's been a good week for us with all the good results. I now have a full week to myself without any poking, prodding and blood tests. I'll catch up on my work and relax a little before I have to go back to Liverpool. I just wish it wasn't so close to Christmas. My doctor says I should be prepared for them to start my treatment. In the medical field, Christmas means nothing.

Happy 16th Birthday Lauren!! Blue Eyes xx

Tuesday 13 December 2011

I've decided to go for a biopsy of my eye again. I got a phone call yesterday telling me that the Professor wants me to have the biopsy again. He wants to be sure it's not a secondary. He thinks that if they can get more tissue this time, the staining will be able to pinpoint exactly where in my body the primary is or establish that the tumour in my eye is the primary. This has not been an easy decision for me to make, given that I've had the procedure before, but after talking it through with my doctor, I agree that, for my own peace of mind and theirs, it's best to test again rather than destroy the tumour and live with the uncertainty. 'What if you get to Easter and then they find something,' the doctor had said. This time last week I was so happy to get clear results, but at the back of my mind I was scared that if nothing was found it might not be as simple as that. As the doctor said, 'Was it best for the primary to be in my eye, or somewhere else that might possibly be easier to treat?' I feel that I'm back at the start again.

I'll have the biopsy again in ten days' time if they think that's my best option. That will be followed by at least two weeks' wait for the results. Please God this one will be more successful. I just hate that it's Christmas. I just want to be okay. I went for an X-ray today of my back – upper and middle lumbar spine.

I feel absolutely sick today. So much for my week of relaxation.

> *Across the fields I can see the radiance of your smile and
> I know in my heart you are there. But the anguish I am feeling makes the
> distance so very far to cross.*
> ~ Deidra Sarault

Sunday 18 December 2011

It's been a tough week. I cried a bit yesterday. Mass cards have been arriving in the post for me, along with the Christmas cards. Everyone's thinking and praying for me. It still feels so surreal. Everything I have stood for seems to be going against me. I'm wishing the days away until next week when I'll be back from Liverpool, home for Christmas and, hopefully, know better what's happening. Yet I'm always telling the kids to stop wishing their lives away.

I have a busy week ahead with lots to sort out before I go away on Thursday morning. The flight is at 8.15 a.m. so I need to be up and ready to go by 6.30 a.m.

We get no guarantees in life. No one can tell me I'll live forever.

I expect – no, I want – to live to a very old age, be there for my kids when they go through their own ups and downs, have kids of their own, and live their dreams. And when I'm asked in my nineties what was the secret to my old age I'll be able to say that I didn't drink or smoke, that I loved music, singing, laughter, love, being loved, hugs and kisses, that I stayed optimistic, worked hard, enjoyed cooking, baking, eating out, my kids, their music, guitar nights, their friends, especially sleepovers, a house full of family and friends, movies, concerts, holidays (jazz in Cork), chats, and homework around the kitchen table. Loved it all – loved it, loved it, loved it.

Don't wait for special days to give flowers or send a card. When you want to do it just do it. Any day can be special. We are all special. Treat yourself. I've often done that, but hey, I'm a Pisces – I deserve to be treated in lots of special and loving ways.

Destruction. Crashes realities exploding in imperfect landings. Ouch. It's my heart that's breaking, for these have been fantasies and my world.
~ Mary Casey

Thursday 22 December 2011

I'm back home from Liverpool. I had a decision to make today and, please God, I've made the right one. I really feel in my heart I have.

Woke up at five o'clock this morning, the flight was on time, and we got to The Royal Liverpool Hospital about half nine. I was taken straight away. I had all my tests and consultations by 10 a.m. and then waited nervously for the Professor.

I was called just after eleven o'clock. 'Here comes trouble,' he said. 'You have everyone in Belfast worried about you.' So I felt right away that it was going to be a better meeting with him than last time. Everyone was there – all his consultants and the surgeon who did my biopsy. That made me a little tense.

He went through the options; the only option I didn't have was to do nothing – we couldn't take the risk that the tumour might grow. He explained that there are three different kinds of tumour: the saint, the petty criminal and the mass murderer. He described mine as the petty criminal, with the potential of becoming a mass murderer if left untreated. After discussing the possibility of a second biopsy he explained that they would have to go deeper into the eye than before and this might cause a certain amount of damage. As the tumour hadn't grown since my last visit he wasn't sure if it was worth putting me through the procedure again. He asked me what I thought. 'Don't look at anyone else. This has to be your decision,' he said.

Petrified and unable to make a decision I told him how I felt, and together we decided not to go for the biopsy. So I was left with the options of proton beam therapy or photo dynamic therapy (PDT). My tumour was close to the optic nerve, so there was a chance that if I went with proton beam therapy followed by radiation treatment, I might lose the sight in my eye. PDT (which uses a cold laser) is a treatment that can be effective on small tumours, so I opted for this less invasive treatment and said my prayers!

The Professor was not as scary this time. The same dark room I went into on my first visit was now white and bright. He was dressed in a grey suit and had a different tone in his voice. I told him that the fluid had gone from my eye. He was excited about this, thinking that maybe it had escaped through the hole made by the biopsy needle, although the surgeon who did the biopsy said he didn't think so. I think myself that it possibly drained away when my eye was numbed before the biopsy. The Professor also discussed the fact that the fluid and the tumour were two separate things, which was what Danny had been thinking.

We were told to go and have some lunch, and I was instructed to drink plenty of water to lessen any pain in my lower back (the dye can sometimes cause this); they would come and get me when they had the treatment set up.

Within an hour the nurse came for me. She took a record of my height and weight, then set up the needle to insert the dye, which would help the laser pick up the tumour in my eye.

There was a slight sensation when the needle went in, but it was okay. I had drops put in to freeze my eyes. Then a circular object was put into my eye to hold it open. The laser treatment began. It lasted eighty-six seconds, and then it was over. I was told to avoid bright lights for twenty-four hours and given a pair of dark glasses and an appointment to come back in two months. Off we went.

We spent an hour in the hospital cafe and then we headed back to the airport for the flight home. We got home about 5.30 p.m. I felt a bit sick, but a cup of tea and some shortbread sorted that out. I just relaxed on the sofa for the rest of the evening, glad that I had finally started on a treatment and hoping it would be successful; I only have three chances for it to work. I was relieved not to be having another biopsy. It was so good to be home to gingerbread men and other baked goodies, thanks to Steven.

When action grows unprofitable, gather information; when information grows unprofitable, sleep

~ Ursula K. LeGuin

Saturday 24 December 2011 – Christmas Eve

'Happy birthday, Grannie Annie.'

Although my grannie is no longer with us, Christmas Eve is all the more special because it is also her birthday. She was very much a mother figure to my two brothers, two sisters and me. I was with her when she took her last breath. I think of her every day. She is the reason a robin visits, and sometimes she sends a song to me via the radio. She is also my earliest musical influence: she played a concertino (squeeze box). I was lucky to grow up with traditional music and ceilis at home. I tried to keep up the tradition by giving my children musical instruments and, hopefully, memories they will carry with them forever.

I cried a lot yesterday, possibly with the relief of it all. Thursday felt as if it was an end to the last year and the start of a different life for me. Whatever happens now with my eye, I won't be the same person ever again. I'll have to make changes, stick with them, carry on with my life and stay positive.

> *Follow your dream …*
> *If you stumble, don't stop*
> *and lose sight of your goal,*
> *press on to the top.*
> *For only on top*
> *Can we see the whole view*
>
> ~ Amanda Bradley

Sunday 25 December 2011 – Christmas Day

It's the first Christmas I haven't cooked Christmas dinner in twenty-four years. It's not the kind of Christmas I had been expecting – me not being a mum. I've lost my way, both as a wife and a mother. I find the changes I've had to make very hard. My wee family have all suffered in different ways, as have I. Let's just hope next year will be a better one.

What we suffer, what we endure … is done by us, as individuals, in private.
~ Louise Bogan

2012

Wednesday 4 January 2012

I got the CD of my consultation in the post today. The team at Liverpool recorded the initial appointments so I would be able to listen to them again – there was so much to take in! After playing it all back I am more confident I made the right decision about going with the PDT treatment. I know now that my eye may not get any better. When they told me at the start that I had central serous retinopathy (fluid under the retina), I hoped it would go away on its own. I was told that if it hadn't gone away within six months they would treat it, so that by February 2012 it would be back to normal.

I now have to accept that this is how my eye will be. My next appointment in Liverpool is on 23rd February, one day after my forty-fifth birthday. I am hoping for a special birthday present – that the treatment will have worked.

It will take me some time to get used to, but I'm thankful to have my sight, even though it is still blurred and I have a little blind spot. I'm not sure if it's maybe a shadow from the tumour. But it could all have been so different.

Once I knew I wanted to be an artist, I had made myself one.
~ Judy Chicago

Tuesday 14 February 2012 – Valentine's Day

I got my MRI breast scan today. This is my last test. It was a deep scan. Although nothing was found on my breast screening back in December they wanted to make completely sure that nothing was starting. This is my fifth dye through my veins; I've lost count of the blood tests. My veins have collapsed, and my body and mind with them. I have spent time over the past month enjoying the company of my youngest son, Brendan, who is home from Cork for a while. I've been resting and trying to get my energy levels up, hoping that the treatment has worked. I will know in just over a week.

Friendship of a kind that cannot easily be reversed tomorrow must have its roots in common interests and shared beliefs.
~ Barbara W. Tuchman

LOok sEE
ThRough KAtiE's EyEs

You look at me and what do you see?
A beautiful person with amazing blue eyes.
Sadness lies behind thought's eyes,
A tumour, but small in size.
The size of a seed they say,
A seed of thought runs through my mind:
Is this it? Am I going to die?

Scary as hell, nowhere to hide,
I have to have treatment if my eye's to survive.
My optic nerve is in the way,
So I opt for laser and to God I pray.

A shadow awaits me as I awake to each new day,
A small reminder of my ordeal.
My tumour cannot be taken away,
But the cancer that lived there will surely die.

Each day when you look at someone, remember,
They might have a secret inside,
And treat them with all the love in your heart.
My eye held a secret, my heart holds the pain.

The cancer is now not the scariest thing in my life,
It's living and not living life right.
So if you have something in your heart you must do,
Go do it with excitement, excitement for YOU!

Everything's pushing me towards a new life,
But the tiredness is keeping me alone in this house.
Keep positive and fight; it's what my mind says.
I'm not sure just where I fit in; the outside's the same,
What has changed is the view from within.

I look out and want more! Is that so wrong?
If I ever break free of this hold on my house,
I will break the fear that holds me inside.
Out in the world is where I belong,
Living my life. Is that so wrong?

Now my shadow reminds me of somewhere in the past.
I got the chance to make better this life that I have.
I feel the excitement of what's yet to come;
I greet it with wisdom and joy in my heart.

What I want might not be what I need,
LOok! sEE, and maybe you will find
A new person! Desperate to have a great life.

You look at me and what do you see?
A beautiful person with amazing blue eyes.
Sadness lives behind thought's eyes
A thirst for life that I cannot deny!
Just because I'm not dying doesn't mean my problems aren't real;
Just because I'm smiling doesn't mean I don't fear.

The eyes tell a story; this is mine.
We are all beautiful and amazing and I hope we stay that way.
Life will get better you'll see, thRough KAtiE's EyEs

Love Katie x
14th Feb 2012

Thursday 23 February 2012

We got to the airport for the flight at 8.15 a.m. My appointment was at 9.30 a.m., so we had a tight race to be there on time. We sat down in the waiting room at 9.30 on the dot and I was called straight away. I was given a nurse to come with me to my different appointments. Then it was time to see the Professor. The tumour has shrunk! It all looks good!

He explained that I could have injections into my eye that might help with the blur. I could get them in Belfast if I felt the need. I decided not to do this unless it got worse. He said he would send me to Belfast for check-ups and I would be seen every six months for two years, then once a year indefinitely, or he would see me back in Liverpool, if necessary. He wished me the best, gave me a dismissal form and I left. When I handed it in to the receptionist, she said, 'I don't mean this in a bad way, but I hope I never see you again.' We laughed. The flight back home was at about four o'clock.

After six months of my world being in a whirl I felt like I had been spat out, and although I was relieved – boy, was I relieved – I couldn't help wondering where I went from here.

This verse has an extra special significance for me. It's the one I'd chosen for the inside cover of my EP a year earlier, before all this started.

I want to dance always, to be good and not evil, and when it is done not to have the feeling that I might have done better.
~ Ruth St. Denis

Saturday 21 April 2012

On Wednesday I have to go back to the Mater Clinic for a check-up. I'm a little nervous about it, but I do feel stronger most days now. I'm still working on my immune system and my energy levels are slowly getting better.

To look backward for a while is to refresh the eye, to restore it, and to render it the more fit for its prime function of looking forward.
~ Margaret Fairless Barber

Wednesday 25 April 2012

At ten o'clock the nurse took me to have a chat and take my blood pressure. My eyes were frozen and their pressure was taken (right: 20; left: 17). Then I went for my scans and an eye examination. My ophthalmologist said, 'Nothing to worry about. It all looks good. The tumour has gone.' She couldn't believe it. Neither could I.

I'd been told at the start that it would shrink, but wouldn't go away. She told me that all my tests had come back clear and that I was now the healthiest person she knew. She checked my eyes again and sent me for more photos to compare them to the first pictures that had been taken. We looked at the pictures on the computer screen. She just couldn't believe it.

She said she would see me again in six months, but to contact her if I had any problems in the meantime.

She told me that the Professor had sent her a letter to say that I might consider injections into my eye, but she didn't think this was necessary as she couldn't see any fluid there. There was still blood in my eye and she explained that the blur I was experiencing was scarring from the biopsy, something that I would hopefully get used to. At least I know what it is; I'm not so frightened of it.

Every day when I wake up it's there as a reminder of my ordeal. This is the strange thing for me because it's in my eye. No matter if my eye is open or closed I see it. I call it my stabiliser – it reminds me not to push myself too hard. When I feel afraid, the blurring gets worse. I can literally see fear in my eyes. When I feel scared my pupils dilate, making the scarring more obvious to me (it's the same when they put the drops into my eyes to test them). Now I understand better what is happening with my eye I've got to a place where I'm not so fearful. The scarring has just become normal. Now, too, I talk about things, rather than hold on to the hurt (better out than an eye, as an old friend used to say).

Everything has its wonders, even darkness and silence, and I learn, whatever state I may be in, therein to be content.
~ Helen Keller

Thursday 26 April 2012

Today a new me is blossoming. The smiles are returning to my world. I am stronger than I ever thought I could be. I'm better now because the cancer has gone from my life. Please God don't let it come back.

Pain is the root of knowledge.
~ Simone Weil

Saturday 28 April 2012

Lauren has planned a benefit night to raise money for the eye clinic at The Royal Liverpool Hospital. Her Blue Eyes Project will be on 27th July 2012, the only night she could get. I've only just realised that that date marks a year since I first had my eye checked at the opticians. Funny how it's worked out.

> *... suffering ... no matter how multiplied ... is always individual.*
> ~ Anne Morrow Lindbergh

Sunday 6 May 2012

I've been reading back through my journal today and added little verses from my book *Each Day a New Beginning*. I bought Karen Casey's little book on my first visit to Cork in August 2010 while leaving my youngest boy there to start a new life. I can't believe how well the quotations in it have corresponded with the things that have been going on in my life. It has given me great encouragement on those days when I hardly knew how I coped. Writing them in my journal today has made me feel very emotional.

> *I stand before you today as a tower of strength, the weight of the world on my shoulders. As you pass through my life, look, but not too close, for I fear I will expose the vulnerable me.*
> ~ Deidra Sarault

Monday 7 May 2012

They say that if you look into someone's eyes you can see into their soul. I wonder what would be seen today if someone looked into my eyes. In the past it would have been pain, and wanting, and needing to know why – why do we hold on to pain when we really need to let it go?

I will learn to let go. I have to for my own sanity. The past few months have taught me a lot about how I should live MY life!

My friend Cathy is running the Belfast Marathon today. She says she will think of me for inspiration when the going gets tough.

> *The eyes tell a story. This is mine.*
> *Love Katie x*

The god Odin took his eye out to gain wisdom. We develop our character while handling painful times. Pain offers wisdom.

2013

Tuesday 7 May 2013

It's a year on from when I last wrote in my journal and I have a new chapter to record. My journey still hasn't reached its conclusion.

I got a big shock when I went for my six-month check-up. Something was wrong. I had to go back to Liverpool on 24th April, one year since I'd been told that the tumour in my eye had gone. It turns out that the tumour is still there. I have to have more treatment in the hope that it will shrink, or I will have to have radiation treatment.

Early in May, ten days after my treatment, I was in Derry for the jazz festival and while sitting relaxing the lady at the reception desk asked if it was okay for a man to sit on the spare sofa beside me and my daughter. He was blind. I didn't tell him anything about me or what a scary place my world had become for me again. He told us a small part of his life story and about his love of jazz music. He had experienced life not by seeing, but by sheer strength of will. We spent just thirty minutes with him that night and we both left inspired by him and his one-man crusade through life, meeting people as he went along and just accepting everyone as a friend – he made quite a few that weekend.

I wonder what he made of us coming all the way to Derry to enjoy the jazz music, but me feeling too insecure to go out and enjoy it – just an hour or so before we met him I had had a panic attack in our room and couldn't get into the lift to come downstairs. I had booked the weekend for us before I knew anything was wrong and I pushed myself to go anyway. I didn't want to give in to my fear. I needed normality, but this time it wasn't quite working for me.

I am shattered from my treatment, and from the worry of it. I will bounce back from this; I have to. But somehow it seems harder this time. Do I get to beat it twice? I just remember my doctor saying, 'What if, in a year, they find something. Then what do you do?'

I have a two-month wait to see if my treatment is working. I'll be back in Liverpool on 4th July, Independence Day. I hope it will be for me.

We tend to think of the rational as a higher order, but it is the emotional that marks our lives. One often learns more from ten days of agony than from ten years of contentment.
~ Merle Shain

Friday 24 May 2013

Today was a really bad day for me. I needed to know what had happened, so I contacted the consultant at the Mater Clinic, who put my mind at ease. It seems that back in April 2012, when I was told that the tumour had gone, what they meant was that activity had stopped and that what I was left with was a shadow, which they call a dormant tumour (non-active tumour). What had happened when I went for my six-month check-up was that they found fluid, which meant that the tumour had become active again.

I have had so much conflicting advice I really don't know what is going on – just that I'm afraid. I have so many questions and not enough answers. I cried a lot today. If only I hadn't been so scared to ask, then my mind wouldn't have conjured up so many frightening thoughts.

It's ironic, but until you free those final monsters within the jungle of yourself, your life, your soul is up for grabs.
~ Rona Barrett

Thursday 4 July 2013

The Professor I usually get for my consultations has retired, so I met my new Professor today. He was nice and explained everything to me, saying that my treatment had worked and that when he measured the tumour it appeared to have no defining edge – it had flattened out – which made it difficult to treat with proton beam therapy. It seems that the photo dynamic therapy is working, and they are hoping to keep it under control in order to avoid radiation treatment and the loss of sight to my eye (or loss of my eye altogether) for as long as possible. He says I will be an oncology patient and be seen in Liverpool for the foreseeable future. He's seeing me again in six months.

One doesn't recognise in one's life the really important moment – until it is too late.
~ Agatha Christie

Friday 5 July 2013

My eldest son, Steven, returned home from Australia today after being away for nine months. It wasn't his first time away from home for work: he went to New Zealand in 2010/2011 to help bring in the harvest. I'm sure he had many emotions, as did I, when for the second time I was told activity had returned to my tumour. I love and encourage my family in all they do, but having Steven so far away has been difficult. I can't believe he's back with us. I'm so thankful to see him again.

I got a double treatment yesterday, which made me feel a little sick. My mouth's dry and I have a slight pain in my back. I've discomfort in my eye, mainly because they freeze it with drops while a circular implement is used to hold the eye open during treatment. It's slightly uncomfortable, but not sore. When the implement is removed, it feels as if it's still there, even when you close your eyes, but this fades after a day or so and with some pain relief. I also noticed for the first time that the dye put through my veins to show up the tumour is black.

> *There are really only two ways to approach life: as victim or as gallant fighter.*
> ~ Merle Shain

A few weeks ago, when my daughter left home to spend a few months in Cork, I found another interesting book. It was about how saying the word F**k can release you from stresses (I found it in the spiritual section of the bookshop!). It made me smile for the simple reason that at the beginning, before I was diagnosed, I couldn't stop saying that word. It was a big shock to my husband and children, who said 'MUM!' because I never usually cursed. After I was diagnosed it just stopped. I know for me there was something in it. I wasn't coping. That word was telling me and everyone around me, something's not right here. I still say it to let off steam every now and then, although looking back, it may have been at the times when activity had returned again. It's not such a bad word, but it's best not overused!

My grannie used to say if you think it, it's as good as saying it, so I'm either not going to think it, or – watch out world – I'll say it!

> *Don't look back. A new day is beginning for us all.*
> *Best of luck with it and make it the best day, you possibly can.*
> ~ Katie McKay

Wednesday 17 July 2013

Today I, Katie McKay, have to accept that I am going to be an oncology patient for the foreseeable future. I must hold on to the positive and keep moving forward in my recovery.

I think it's a good time to pass my words on to someone else. I know everyone's experience will be different, but I very much hope it helps you in this strange world you now find yourself in.

The problem is not merely one of woman and career, woman and home, woman and independence. It is more basically: how to remain whole in the midst of the distractions of life; how to remain balanced, no matter what centrifugal forces tend to pull one off centre; how to remain strong, no matter what shocks come in at the periphery and tend to crack the hub of the wheel.
~ Anne Morrow Lindbergh

Tuesday 23 July 2013

When we were thinking of ways to raise money for the Ocular Oncology Unit at The Royal Liverpool Hospital we thought of having a movie night. We would book a movie theatre – hopefully get a good deal on the rate – and enjoy a good movie while raising money for research to help improve the valuable work already being done at the unit.

Research has made it possible for me to keep my eye while all the time new and amazing treatments are developed to ensure we are given the very best care. I think it is pretty amazing, the efforts that go into saving an eye. It is also thanks to people who donate their eyes so this valuable work can happen. The Royal Liverpool is a teaching hospital and everyone coming through those doors, past and present, also contributes in some way to making future research possible. Indeed, looking back, this is the reason so many nurses and ophthalmologists are present for the consultations – they're there to learn from each other. Had I thought of this at the time, it wouldn't have been so scary. With hindsight, I also know that I made a mistake back on my first visit to Liverpool by not accepting the help of a psychiatrist. I thought I could make it through with the help of my family, but at the beginning I kept a lot from them, and as activity returned I pulled away, not wanting them to get close in case they were going to lose me. As time went on I did ask for help, but I could only get it in Liverpool. That kind of help wasn't available at the Mater Eye Clinic. My doctor suggested counselling, but it wouldn't have been specific to my eye problems and I didn't think it would be much help. Liverpool seemed so far away, so writing out my thoughts and feelings freed me up in many ways, and helped me get through it. We all face different outcomes as we walk through the doors of The Royal Liverpool Hospital for the first time and sit in the waiting room. It's where patients' common thoughts and fears meet, although very often we don't speak to each other.

Sight is part of our energy, and the retina is the only place in the body where the arteries and veins can be seen. Everywhere else is covered with skin, making our eyes our greatest asset and worthy of our constant care and protection.

The Ocular Oncology Unit in Liverpool treats people from all over the UK and further afield – even as far away as Australia. So if you're from Liverpool you are indeed very lucky – although you may not think it if you have just been diagnosed.

> *For this is wisdom: to live, to take what fate, or the Gods, may give.*
> ~ Laurence Hope

Thursday 24 October 2013

Today is a big day for me. It's exactly two years since I was told I had a tumour in my eye and began treatment. On 19th October 2012 I had gone into a recording studio for the first time to start recording a full album of country songs; I decided I just wanted to sing. Tonight I am releasing my 13-track CD, *It Gets Better*. It's a different kind of scary – a good scary.

I stood and looked out at everyone who had come to support me. It was a full house filled with proud faces. The nerves left me, and all because a friend said, 'Smile. I don't know you without a smile.'

When I was standing waiting to sing my first song I remembered that this night two years ago Danny was driving me home from the airport and I was wondering how I was going to tell my mum, my daughter Lauren, and my boys what had happened. In the space of a few hours everything had changed. Now I'm hoping and praying that it gets better.

> *Music washes away from the soul the dust of everyday life ...*
> ~ Berthold Auerbach

Friday 25 October 2013

The whole experience has been a setback for me, a massive shock. It was tough. I was more afraid than I have ever been. The best and only thing I could do was carry on with my recording, give myself something to focus on. I kept my recording dates, added more and sang lots. I was determined to be finished and standing in front of everyone singing. I wanted to take the date – 24th October – and change it to a good memory. Kick cancer and the fear it had given me in the butt.

Back in March I had sent a couple of my tracks to George Jones at Downtown Radio. I hadn't told him anything about me – I just sent the tracks and he invited me in for a live interview on 16th September 2013. His researcher, Kirsten Elder, phoned me a couple of days before the interview to ask some brief questions about me so George could prepare for the interview. Then I had to explain why I had just started to record. It was a very surreal day. I sang Jenn Bostic's song 'Jealous of the Angels', a song I had recorded a week before Chrisy, my nephew, died (on 24th February 2013).

I had been at Downtown the previous year on Candy Devine's Sunday morning show after sending her my journal and the EP asking for advice on what to do. I was very surprised when she invited me in for a live interview and encouraged me to keep writing and singing. It had taken me a year to get back. As I shook hands with George I immediately relaxed and enjoyed the whole experience. That night, Big T played my song on Downtown Country for the first time; he had borrowed it from George.

George rang me later to say he'd had such an amazing response to my recording, with listeners texting and phoning in, that he had sent my recording of the song to Jenn Bostic in Nashville, and I was to expect her to be in touch. Again, I was overwhelmed by the generosity of people. The confidence I had been given from that day I will not forget.

Next day, I was in the Cancer Centre at the City Hospital, Belfast, being told I had to have more tests over the next couple of weeks. With the date for the release of my CD *It Gets Better* in a month's time it looked like time was not on my side. Next day I was in a field having my photo taken for my first album cover. It was a weird time for me, going from one extreme to another.

Then on Friday at the end of that week I got an email from Jenn Bostic thanking me for recording her song. A strange coincidence happened when Jenn sent me the email about my recording of 'Jealous of the Angels'. She told me her dad passed away on 16th February when Jenn was just a little girl. I recorded the song on the 15th February (2013) and was so excited with how it turned out I spent all of the next day (16th February) singing it. I even played it down the phone to my son, Steven, who had called me from Australia while I was out shopping. The song is precious to me for so many reasons, not least because I really felt it as I recorded it, and every time I sing it. Jenn also allowed me to put part of her message to me on the sleeve of my first album. I would never have imagined any of this happening. It made my first album very special.

Then I got a phone call from Robert Skates of Downtown Radio to ask if I would do a radio interview by phone on Sunday morning for his show. CRAZY WEEK! The funny thing was I had been listening to Robert's daytime show a couple of years previously and I'd entered a competition he was running to win tickets to see Dolly Parton. I hadn't been able to get a ticket they had sold out so quickly. I'd never entered a competition before, but made a promise to myself that if I won I would sing – someday I would find the courage and I would sing. Guess what – I won! Now was the time to tell Robert my story. He loved it! Thanks, Robert. Almost every time you played my track 'Jealous of the Angels' I got an order for the CD.

The next two weeks were tough. In between tests, I was recording two days a week, trying to get my CD finished. I got my test results and everything looked good but – there was always a 'but' – there was a query on my neck. I would need an ultrasound and a biopsy. With my CD release night only two weeks away, I tried to forget about it and make my final preparations for the release, hoping I wouldn't get my appointment until after that night, as it would affect my voice.

Love has the quality of informing almost everything—even ones work.
~ Sylvia Ashton-Warner

Thursday 20 November 2013

After a two week wait I got a clear result!

Two days after I got my results, I was back at Downtown Radio. George invited me to meet Jenn Bostic, who was over from Nashville on tour. She was lovely. We chatted for a bit and had our photos taken. She invited me to her concert on the Saturday night. Then I was asked to stand in for her at an event on the Sunday in Belfast for survivors of suicide, where I was to sing 'Jealous of the Angels'. Talk about being thrown in at the deep end! I can't thank George enough for all he's done. He has helped change my life.

Now for the next thing on my bucket list – finishing my music video!

Continuous effort—not strength or intelligence is the key to unlocking our potential.
~ Liane Cordes

Tuesday 31 December 2013 – New Year's Eve

I started recording my second album today. Exactly a year earlier, we had spent the evening out celebrating the New Year. With us was my uncle, who was also my godfather, a father-figure in my life (he gave me away on my wedding day twenty-five years ago). But he didn't make it home and passed away on 3rd January 2013 at the age of eight-three. So singing today was emotional for a lot of reasons.

I had this overwhelming need to be at the New Year celebration that night. Early in the evening I had contacted my cousin to see if he could get us tickets. I don't know what made me feel something was wrong, but it was my mum I was concerned about. When we arrived everyone was surprised, especially my mum and my uncle. During the meal I noticed something different about my uncle. I remember saying to

Mum that I would take him up for a dance – he loved to dance. It was while we were dancing that I had this really strange feeling. He sat in his seat most of the night, everyone coming over to him for a chat, which was heartbreaking to watch because he was usually the one covering the room, either chatting or dancing. He rarely sat still and always enjoyed nights out. Before I left to go home I kissed him and said 'Night night.' Those were my last words to him; they were words I had never said to him before.

On 9th November 2012, my twenty-six-year-old nephew Christopher – Chrisy – was given the news we all dreaded, he was told he didn't have long to live. He had been suffering from cancer (Ewing's sarcoma) for the past six years, losing his right arm to this horrendous disease, which then spread to his lungs.

At the same time, all the family on my husband's side was caring for our dad who had liver cancer – well, technically he was my father-in-law, but he came into my life the same year I lost my dad so he became my dad too and had been for the past twenty-seven years. On 28th November 2012 he passed away at the grand old age of ninety-three. On his first year anniversary I had a white feather on my back; I still have the feather and him watching over me.

With the first anniversary of Chrisy's death in February, I released a track called 'Adam's Song' and the money will be donated to Chrisy's memorial fund. The last time I spoke to Chrisy was two days before he died, and it was my birthday.

The most amazing thing happened on the day Chrisy passed away. We had been at the hospital from about one o'clock. Chrisy's sister Julieann, who will always be a daughter to me, had phoned us to come to the hospital. When we arrived he had been unresponsive all morning. Lauren stayed with me at the hospital. There were a lot of visitors that day;

we were going in and out and he never responded. Julieann asked me if I thought she should bring her two daughters to the hospital. They were the reason Chrisy had made it through Christmas. I told her that if she wanted them to be there then yes, let them come. Alesha was first to arrive and was only there for a short time. Then the doctor told us he didn't think Chrisy would make it until the morning; we were welcome to stay if we wanted. We had just been to the shop for food and drink to get us through the night when Olivia arrived. Olivia is the eldest of Julieann's girls and was three at the time. She was excited to see everyone and went around giving everyone hugs. Then Julieann took her in to see Chrisy and with one deep breath he was gone. He had waited for Olivia to come. Leaving his sweet nieces was his hardest battle.

On the Wednesday of the week before, I had been to his home to visit him. As I lay on the bed beside him he said, 'Last night I ate right through my arm band, so they're turning up my morphine today.' He was so, so brave. I remember asking Lauren afterwards, 'What do you take from death?' She had lost three family members in such a short period of time – Chrisy, her grandad and my uncle – and she was only seventeen. She said, 'How people keep on going. They pick themselves up and keep on going.'

It was a precious time for me because we got to say goodbye to Chrisy that night. He will never be forgotten. I have so many questions, but only God knows the reasons why.

Music is the one thing that gets me through. Music fills the gap for me in what can be a scary day. It has given this especially difficult year a purpose. If I can make someone happy with my music then it's an added bonus.

In the process of growing to spiritual maturity, we all go through many adolescent stages.
~ Miki L. Bowen

2014

Tuesday 13 May 2014

I went to the oncology unit for the latest results after eight months of worry. I now have no more tests for six months at either oncology or the eye clinic. It has been a hectic few months since 25th September 2013, when I had a full body scan. I had been given an injection of radiation and left to lie still for one hour, then taken and scanned for forty-five minutes from head to knees, then turned around and scanned from knees to the top of my toes for fifteen minutes. This has been my scariest scan to date. The following week I had a MRI scan.

The results of the full body scan showed up a hotspot on my neck, on which I had a biopsy on 7th November with a clear result. These tests were all as a result of activity that resumed in the tumour in my eye in April 2013.

Just before Christmas 2013 I had been called into the doctor's. A hotspot had been found in my MRI scan too. After a bit of confusion and another appointment in January, I had to attend ENT. A hotspot, as they call it, was found in my ear – 'cell activity'. On Tuesday 4th March, I had another CT scan, this time to include my temporal bones. I got the results on Friday 4th April 2014.

It was a tough day. The doctor was lovely – he almost made me cry – but I was going off to record another song so I had to hold back; I had to be good at not showing my true feelings. For the first time a professional made me realise what an ordeal I had been through. He gave me the result. Then he said, 'You look worried. Is that why you have company?' (my daughter Lauren was with me). That was the moment I almost cried. He took both my hands and said, 'It's all good. Your tests are clear.' Then he told his colleague that I had a cordial tumour in my eye and asked me to explain how I knew and what the treatment process was. He asked how they did the biopsy in my eye. 'I hope they knocked you out for that,' he said, but I had to tell him no. He took both my hands again and asked if he and his colleague could take a look. I will never forget his kindness to me that day. He said to come back if I ever had a problem with my ears. He said he would remember me because I was unusual.

Within an hour I was back in the recording studio getting ready to record my next track 'Tonight the heartache's on me'. I finished recording that day at five o'clock and went straight home for a much needed bath and a much needed cry.

Just before the doctor had called me in, Downtown Radio was playing in the waiting room. 'I'm Alright' came on. Lauren and I looked at each other. 'I bet that's the first time you've heard that song on the radio,' I said and she just smiled at me in the way she usually does when a coincidence like this happens to me. The funny thing was that when I came to ENT for my first appointment in January, I was going off to record 'I'm Alright' after the appointment. That kind of thing happens to me a lot and I love it. I am so relieved I can't tell you. It has been a very intense time. I also put my first music video up on YouTube, which made my day. Tomorrow I will be singing on the Downtown Radio stage at the Balmoral Show, another ask by George Jones.

Your sense of what will bring happiness is so crude and blundering. Try something else as a compass. Maybe the moralists are right and happiness doesn't come from seeking pleasure and ease.
~ Joanna Field

Friday 16 May 2014

I finished the last track on my second album and when I noticed the quote for the day, I realised that it expressed my thoughts perfectly for this day. I knew it would come to represent something significant and it has. It's a great day for me in this strange world I now find myself in.

I am having a few weeks break before I start my third album. With all the uncertainty, my best option is to get as much music recorded as I can. I want to have a good mix of songs ready so that when the time comes to get out there, I will be prepared – I hope.

Given that I have no tests for six months I am looking forward to a more relaxed period of recording.

It is only the women whose eyes have been washed clear with tears who get the broad vision that makes them little sisters to the world.
~ Dorothy Dix

2015

Wednesday 4 February 2015

I can't begin to imagine the kind of skill it takes to go inside an eye and stitch four button-type markers around a tumour. To think the hands of a man can do such delicate work. I am truly blessed!

I had my surgery on the morning of 16th January, a Friday. I was the only one on the Professor's list for that day. I had had all my pre-ops the day before, so we had flown over on Thursday morning and stayed in the hotel to be ready for my morning admission.

We went to the movies on Thursday evening to see *The Theory of Everything*, an amazingly inspirational movie. Then we had a late dinner because I had to fast for the next morning. It was a lovely evening as we walked back to the hotel through Liverpool city centre. It looks so beautiful, I thought to myself, as if I was only seeing it for the first time. I didn't want to think too much about what I had in front of me the next day and was trailing my feet, knowing that as soon as I got back to the hotel the day would be over and I'd be closer to this day that I had been dreading.

It took me a long time to get my bearings that day after I had had my surgery. I was taken to the theatre at 9 a.m. I woke up, tears running down my face, from the enormity of it all. I had got to the other side of my surgery and relief washed through me. Tea and toast was given and I returned to my chair in the admissions ward at about 11.30 a.m. A bed would have been nice while I recovered, especially as I was having to go for a flight home later that evening, and there was only me that day after all. I hope that wasn't the reason why.

I slipped in and out of sleep, waking in pain and more tears. I wasn't crying; it was just tears running down my face. The nurse asked me what was wrong. 'I'm in pain,' I said. 'Did I not get any pain relief? I've a good pain threshold, but something's wrong.' I was given two painkillers and checked again later. But it was still no better and I was aware that I had a flight to catch. I needed to leave the hospital by 3 p.m.

I was taken to be seen by an ophthalmologist. It turned out that my cornea had been scratched during surgery. She said the pain was excruciating, but that it goes completely within twenty-four hours. Some painkillers were required and we headed to the airport. In the taxi the pain hit again and the tears came. Now I understood why I had tears; it felt like I was being stabbed in the eye and it made my eyes water. Getting on to the plane we had to walk out through a hail storm, then up the steps at the back of the plane to get to our seats. I hit my head off the baggage compartment. Ouch! Once I was in my seat the tears came for real. They were tears of relief. I knew I would soon be back home recovering and getting ready for the next step: proton beam therapy – radiation!

My eye is making slow but steady progress. Having the steroid drops put in was extremely painful, bringing tears to my eyes – and to Danny's, as he put them in for me at the start when I couldn't open my eye to put them in myself. He has been a great support to me since my surgery. I really needed him and he was there for me. I had six stitches in the front of my eye where the surgeon made the incision. Three have dissolved;

three are still there. I have a tightness in my eye. As each stitch dissolves there is great relief.

We flew over to Liverpool on Monday 26th January. We got a bus to the city centre, a train out to the Wirral and then a taxi to the hotel. The next day we went to Clatterbridge Cancer Hospital where I had my mask made in preparation for my radiation treatment, which is to start on 10th February.

I was taken into the room where I would have my radiation treatment. My photo was taken, and then I was seated in a specially designed chair that adjusts to the various types of people and positions of their tumour. There was a frame on the front of the chair, which I had to put my head into, and a mask template made of a soft white mesh was put over my face. Once the mesh hardened this was my mask. It was then inserted into the frame and secured while I bit on a mould that I'd made at the start of the process. This was to keep me in the same position for each day of treatment. A patch was put on the mask to block out the eye not having treatment; adjustments and measurements were made. I was shown an x-ray of the positions of the markers. I asked how they had put them in; I hadn't been brave enough to ask on the day of my surgery. The nurse said, 'Let's just say you'll be glad you were put out for the procedure.' I then went to meet my oncologist, who says they have a 95–98% success rate, but this is my last chance to save my eye. They will hit it hard with a high dose of radiation. There is a chance I may lose my sight. I will know within the next twelve to eighteen months. Then we got a taxi back to Liverpool for our flight home. It's been a tough few months and still counting.

I had a breakdown moment when I got home. The stark reality of it all, the sense of creeping closer to my last hope. Lauren was there with two loving arms. She just let me cry and I needed that, plus my arsenicum , which has helped me cope with my fears these past few years.

Genius is the talent for seeing things straight. It is seeing things in a straight line without any bends or breaks or aberrations of sight, seeing them as they are, without any warping of vision.

~ Maude Adams

Saturday 7 February 2015

I am forever amazed by the angst of life – what drives us, how we keep going. The incredible recovery of the body and of the mind – of my precious eye. Although I have fought with this constantly recurring disease, the story has come full circle for me now. How do the pieces of our lives stay together? How many times do I get to fall apart? It has brought me back to a place of fear too many times, and yet when I'm in the depths of it all I still feel blessed.

On 13th November 2014 I attended the Royal for my six-month check-up. At first my appointment was going well, and then I was sent back because the scan hadn't been taken of the correct part of my eye. I did have a slight fear, I can't tell where it came from, but I had been for my six-month test results on the Tuesday at oncology, so it was a worrying time. Although those results were clear I had a feeling about my eye. So when I was told that the tumour had slightly thickened I just knew I was heading back to Liverpool. I had my longest wait yet from Liverpool to get my appointment. I had hoped this was because they were not concerned, but unfortunately the sheer volume of patients means that we are having to wait longer to be seen.

I got chatting to a patient that day. She had had the proton beam therapy and was back for a review. She was also nervous, expecting to be told she would lose her eye – she was sure of it. I was also feeling that perhaps this was my fate. She told me that she had been shown an artificial eye back when she was first told she had a tumour. She said that they take out your eye and put the new eye in straight away so the muscle takes on the new eye and it moves much like your own eye. I was very relieved to hear this. I can't tell you what it meant to me. I was called in for a chat before seeing the Professor, but when I returned she had been called for her appointment and had been taken out through the other door, so I never spoke to her again.

I accepted defeat on the 4th December 2014 when I sat in the same chair I had sat in three years earlier (and, of course, many times since) to be told that my treatment wasn't working. For my own sanity I had to stop, go for surgery and the proton beam therapy treatment. So for the second time I was taken out through the other door into the room where I was given information and dates were arranged.

It was 6 p.m. before we finally left the eye clinic. With Christmas and New Year looming I didn't want to think I was heading into another year with appointments and tests, never mind surgery and radiation treatment, all of it back in Liverpool. That week in February was going to be difficult, having to be away from everyone.

Too late for our flight home we stayed in a hotel. I needed a break from thinking. I sent messages home saying I needed more treatment. I didn't say what kind – I wanted to do that face-to-face. As a family we would have to be strong again. I can see it's harder for everyone each time.

We went for dinner. With it being December, the tables were all set for Christmas. We ordered two Christmas dinners and then pulled our crackers. Danny got playing cards. Me? I got an eye patch! It must have been payback time from Chrisy because I had promised him I was going to buy him a comb with no teeth when his hair all came out. Danny and I laughed properly for the first time in weeks. Then he looked up to the heavens and said, 'What are you trying to do to us?'

However confused the scene of our life appears, however torn we may be who now do face that scene, it can be faced, and we can go on to be whole.
~ Muriel Rukeyser

Thursday 26 February 2015

It's two weeks since I had my radiation treatment and apart from having a problem with my eye pressure, which I'm told is a side effect of the steroid drops I have to put in my eye after the radiation treatment, I am doing okay.

The proton beam therapy allows the radiation to work in my eye for four to six weeks, but only in the eye – it doesn't affect any other parts of my body. It's quite amazing really.

Lauren came with me for the week. I'm sure she was nervous, like me – especially of this part, as it is the last hope to save my eye. I was very afraid and very aware of my worries. The treatment itself was not the worst thing. My eye felt very wet and strangely odd. Having my eyelid taped up was sore, but having my eyelashes taped was worse – well, to be honest having the tape removed from my eyelashes was the most horrible feeling. On the first day I thought my eyelashes had all come out!

The care I received at the Centre was great – it was so warm and friendly. During my radiation treatment we spent the week in a hotel in the Wirral, along with thirteen other people undergoing treatment. A taxi came to take us for our appointments – one out, one in. I don't know what people must have thought seeing us coming back with a patch on one eye. It felt so weird. I did lose sense of the real world for the week. Unlike me, most of the other patients at the hotel were at the beginning of their journey. We all had something in common; we were all there for the same reason, each of us wanting a good result and someone to talk to.

Happiness is a by-product of an effort to make someone else happy.
~ Gretta Brooker Palmer

Monday 23 March 2015

I had my six-week check today at The Royal Victoria Hospital with my ophthalmologist. It will be six weeks tomorrow since I started the proton beam therapy radiation treatment. I'm disappointed to learn that they found no change to the tumour and that I have fluid back in my eye. A letter will go to the Professor to see what he thinks. I know the radiation is still doing something. I can feel a little discomfort, and just in the last couple of weeks a burn on my eyelid. I can say I am very aware of my eye some days, more so than others. It feels bulgy, a little swollen, and has been like this since the surgery. I'm hoping it's early days, but I'm disappointed that there isn't even a small change to the tumour. Positivity reigns again and I go home hoping I haven't gone through all this for nothing.

On occasion I realise it's easier to say the serenity prayer and take that leap of faith than it is to continue doing what I'm doing.

~ S.H.

Serenity Prayer
God give me the serenity
To accept the things I cannot change;
Courage to change the things I can;
And the wisdom to know the difference.

Friday 27 March 2015

I don't really know how to help myself. Should I rest all the time? That's an impossible task for me.

I miss my work, the adrenalin rush from a good work-out; even yoga is missing from my life just now. Oh, to get stuck into a good spring clean now that spring has arrived. I miss recording. It had given me a purpose, a structure. Having to take time out from my music is so very hard. I am missing it from my life.

Ten weeks on since my surgery and I still can't wear make-up on my eyes because of the radiation burn on my eyelid. I have hit the depression button quite a number of times over the years, but more so in the last few months. This is my hardest battle. But it's more the loneliness that having surgery to your eye brings, as if it has changed me. I just needed company in those first couple of weeks while I waited for my eye to recover a little bit, for the redness to go and the stitches to ease.

In the beginning I wasn't sure if my eye would return to normal. As you can imagine it has taken a bit of a battering.

It takes time, love and support to find peace with the restless one.
~ Deidra Sarault

Dedicated to my daughter Lauren (Lori)

Growing up, I wanted to be a long-distance lorry driver. My cousin had an articulated lorry. He would come to visit Mum, and the lorry would be parked outside our house. I loved everything about it, from its size to what it represented – freedom, purpose, colour and adventure in my dull world.

That's what my Lori is to me, from the size of her imagination to what she represents – freedom, purpose, colour and adventure in a world of love she shares with me. She is part of the strong woman that I am, and I am part of the many strong women on both sides of my family.

During this journey my strength has sometimes left me; emotions have clouded my days. But emotions are what make us women. Set aside your tears, sweet girl, you have lived there too long.

Love Mum xx
13 April 2015

Tuesday 21 April 2015

I'm driving down the road, singing along, trying to distract my mind from what might be wrong. I left the dinner on the stove – well, I did tell Danny it would be ready in twenty minutes. Then at 4.30 p.m. I got a call from my doctor's reception:

'The doctor wants you to come in,' she said.

'Okay,' I said panicking a little. 'When?'

'Now, if that's possible.'

'Okay, I'll leave now. It'll take me twenty minutes to get there.'

'That's fine. See you then.'

So I just fed the dog and left, telling no one.

Earlier in the day I had been to the hospital for an ultrasound of my abdomen and pelvis. Something had to be wrong if the doctor had got the result back already. I went straight into the doctor's room when I got there. She explained that they had reported on my ultrasound and a 3 cm by 2 cm mass had been found on my right kidney. I tried to keep myself composed so as not to miss what she was saying. It might not be serious but they recommended a CT scan. She told me to try not to worry!

I smiled, thanked her and went back to the car. Music was playing but it was no good; I wasn't able to hold back the tears. I've held on to my eye too long. I should just have made them take it. I remembered the doctor saying, 'Just tell them to take your eye when they wanted to biopsy it for the second time.' But I couldn't bring myself to tell them to do that. I always took the advice of the Professor in Liverpool, knowing that he and his team were doing their best for me. If at anytime they had said 'We have to take your eye', I wouldn't have questioned it. Now I was so scared I would have taken it out myself.

I went for an appointment yesterday to have my eye checked. My ophthalmologist is sending scans and photos to the Professor in Liverpool. There's still no change. I desperately want to know what's going on. Around Easter time I had been in a lot of pain in my stomach and back. I could barely walk or sit, but it was impossible to get an appointment over the holiday. Looking back now I really should have gone to A&E. I took painkillers and lay down with a hot water bottle. The pain was so bad I could barely breathe. It eased a little over the weekend and I got an appointment after the holidays. By that time it was a week since the pain had first started.

The doctor sent me for a full blood picture, a breath test to rule out a tummy bug, some x-rays and a bowel test. The bloods were taken on the Tuesday, and on Thursday I was asked to phone the doctor. All the blood tests were clear except one, she told me. But there was something questionable about my kidney function test so they wanted me to go for an ultrasound. 'Oh, I'm due for my six-month check at oncology on Thursday,' I said, 'and it happens to be an ultrasound of my liver.' But she said she would refer me for the ultrasound anyway and if I got an appointment before that to go to it. This did worry me – it would be pretty quick to get an appointment in a week, never mind before that.

When I returned from my eye appointment on Monday the letter had came in the post: the appointment was for the next day. So I was nervous already, and then getting a result so quickly afterwards – well, I'm very scared. Now Danny and I have another secret to keep for now, until we know better what's going on.

Thursday 23 April 2015

I'm going to the doctor's for a kidney function test, then catching the train at noon to the City Hospital for my 1.30 appointment to get an ultrasound of my liver. The radiologist looked over the letter the doctor had given me, noting the results of my ultrasound on Tuesday. She took a copy for the doctor and then did my examination. Her colleague also examined me and the results were sent through to the consulting doctor for that day, who was now looking at two sets of photos, one showing a 3 cm by 2 cm mass, and another showing nothing, and reported on by two radiologists. What was going on? Everyone was confused. The radiologist was so kind to me. 'I'm sure there's nothing for you to worry about,' she said. 'It looks like a shadow. I hope this has put your mind at rest, but the doctor still wants you to go for the CT scan because of your history and to be completely sure.'

I went to the cafe for a cup of tea, having fasted for seven hours because of the test, although food doesn't seem to stay with me for long. I'm at the point where tea and toast is the only food that doesn't run straight through me. Oh, and chocolate – I can eat chocolate. It seems to settle my tummy, strangely enough, because the way I'm feeling at the minute it should make me sick. I walked back to get the train home. There's a funny thing about going for appointments on your own – people smile, say hello and chat to you. They don't know me, I don't have to be me for a bit. But if I take someone with me I'm always more aware that they're on edge. It can be very difficult. On my own I can digest things better, analyse what's happening. It's hard to explain, but the thought that I have worried people is somehow harder than being on my own with it. Danny, bless him, never says the right thing because there very rarely are words; sometimes silence and holding my hand says more. I'm back home now, and, like me, Danny can't work out what's going on.

Friday 24 April 2015

I got two letters in the post this morning: one from the Professor in Liverpool, and one from the Appointments Department. I need to phone them to arrange my CT scan. Hopefully, I won't have long to wait. Now I know that what has been happening to my eye is in keeping with the proton beam therapy. My eye is suffering from oedema/fluid. That explains why I feel pressure and swelling in my eye sometimes. Since the treatment I have been very aware of my eye. I am disappointed not to have been given this information a month ago when my ophthalmologist had written with concerns about the swelling. I should have been made aware this could happen when I was given the proton beam therapy. It would have saved me a lot of anxiety this past few weeks. It has been especially worrying because having fluid in my eye in the past has always meant activity in the tumour has started again.

My ophthalmologist saw me on Monday, but hadn't heard back from Liverpool, so she sent over photos and scans because she is still concerned with my progress. It appears that my tumour has thickened slightly since she saw me back in November 2014. I'm thinking that it may have grown while I was waiting for my surgery, and although she had said there was no change when she saw me for my first check-up back on 23rd March, I'm wondering if she said that just because she didn't want to worry me. I'm sure today, having received the letter, her mind will be more at ease.

This night last week I was at my cousin's birthday party. I sang a few songs and enjoyed a great family night. No one knew the turmoil I was in. I've become good at hiding behind a smiling face. Having come to the end of this crazy week, I'm glad Lauren has left to live with her brother in Cork. Had she been at home I wouldn't have been able to avoid telling her. Because the boys don't live at home with us it's been much easier for them not to be aware of every detail. I'm scared more times than not. Most of the time it takes all my strength to go out and face people. It's only on reflection that I can put myself at ease enough to try and explain to anyone what's happening. Being on my own with it makes me feel I can accept it or have some control of my feelings, even if it's only to scream out loud. Mostly I'm screaming inside, not knowing how to be this person coping with this horrendous thing that may or may not be taking over my body.

Tuesday 28 April 2015

My appointment for the CT scan came today. After the urgency following the abnormal result in my liver function test it will be three weeks before I get the CT scan, and then a further wait for the results. ANNOYED! And if I hear 'No news is good news' one more time … Grrrr! No news is worrying; for me it usually means another test.

I'm back to getting on with my life. I've been in touch with Paul, who has been recording me, and booked myself in to the studio to start recording before the end of the year. I need to get back to singing. I'm missing my music so much.

Wednesday 6 May 2015

Got my letter this morning. The Professor has brought my date forward, so I'm going back to Liverpool in three weeks. My world is feeling a little smaller and is crushing my chest. I had my appointment yesterday at oncology, and as they couldn't give me a positive result because of the query over my kidney, I was examined and a blood test taken for my liver function. This showed up an abnormality that led to the ultrasound and a CT scan, which I go for on Friday.

Thursday 7 May 2015

I hit a wall yesterday. I just cried the day and night away. Being awake for most of the night, I decided on the new tracks I wanted to record. I'm going to do something a bit different this time around. I drifted off to sleep somewhere around 4 a.m.! But I haven't totally wasted the day. I'd have been happier if I had written something myself, but my head's too full of worry to concentrate. It has been a few months now since new words have given me a song.

Friday 8 May 2015

I went for my appointment this morning only to find it was a consultation on the results of my CT scan, not to have the CT scan itself – a waste of time for both of us, as was apparent on the consultant's face and, I'm sure, on mine. Although he said he thought there was nothing to worry about, they want to do the CT scan to totally rule it out. The kidney looked good. It was in the pole where the mass appeared to be and if this was the case they could operate to remove it. He asked me what my symptoms were. I explained that I had pain across my stomach, down my right side and in my back. He said that it sounded more like a gallbladder problem, which was what I had thought myself, or that it was a stone which I might have passed. He also said that cancer in the kidney didn't have symptoms. That was a little worrying to hear. So I have to travel back on Tuesday for the CT scan, and not for the first time since I started having tests, I'm beyond exhausted by it all.

Monday 11 May 2015

Mum phoned today. I decided to tell her some of what's going on, hoping above all that I am having my last test – well, at least for six months. I'm having the CT scan tomorrow, so she only has one night to think about it. I also told her that I was going to Liverpool earlier than I was supposed to. I had been trying to avoid the conversation if only for another day until I had my scan over. Now that I've told Mum, I sent a message to Brendan and Lauren and told Steven and Darren later after they came in from work. I still haven't told them why I was having the CT scan or that I might have to tell them something worse.

Tuesday 12 May 2015

The CT scan is over and now the wait begins. My phone rang at about two o'clock. It was the hospital. I panicked for a moment, but they were phoning to change an appointment I had at Antrim Hospital, from the 20th to the 28th May, but I am going to Liverpool that day. So with a new appointment date of 3rd June, I'm heading into another month and more appointments. Once my panic had subsided, I decided to relax and try to keep positive.

Wednesday 13 May 2015

I jumped into the pickup and went to the Balmoral Show with Danny and Darren, who were going to show sheep. The seven o'clock news came on just as Danny started the engine: 'A young man's family are having to raise funds to send his sister for treatment for pancreatic cancer. She is fifteen-weeks pregnant.' Her cancer had been undiagnosed, even though she had been complaining of pain in her stomach and back. My already nervous tummy was doing flips. I had decided to take my mind off the tests and get away from it all by enjoying a few days at the show, but now I was staring out the window with a new fear taking over my thoughts. I enjoyed the day, chatting, laughing and meeting Adrian from Downtown Radio who really enjoys my music. I was interviewed by Big T for the Country Show on Downtown later that evening. It really took my mind off waiting for my results for a few hours.

Thursday 14 May 2015

Another day at the Balmoral Show and plenty of laughs. Although the weather wasn't as good as the previous day, the crowds were just as big. There was a little more country music and chats and then my Show days were over. I didn't know if

I would make it for the three days. My eye was quite sore and very bloodshot after just the first day. But I was able to wear my sunglasses; otherwise I wouldn't have gone at all.

So we made our way home. Danny and Steven were going back for the last day. Then the sheep would come home and the show would be over for another year. I arrived home to a letter from my ophthalmologist to say that my appointment in Liverpool might be changed to July because there had been a crossover with letters between Belfast and Liverpool. I give up! Is there anyone in this process who realises I have a family and a life that I am trying to get on with. Having waited so long to tell everyone about the appointment so as not to upset them, I now have to tell them that the date has changed. I'm on the verge of a breakdown. I need to wait for confirmation from Liverpool before I can say for sure.

Saturday 16 May 2015

Another day, another appointment letter and another CT scan – this time with a contrast dye. I have to be at the City Hospital on Wednesday for nine in the morning. It's a good thing my other appointment for the 20th was cancelled. I'm not quite sure why I have to have another scan so soon. It's only been a week since my last CT scan at the Causeway Hospital. Maybe they've referred me back. But it's Saturday so I can't contact anyone to find out why!

Monday 18 May 2015

I couldn't get through by phone to oncology or Liverpool. I left a message for the Professor's secretary to let me know if my appointment still stands. I phoned my GP to see if she had heard anything about my CT scan and if she knew why I was being given another one. She had got the result and my kidney was okay, but there was a blockage on the pole so she had referred me on to urology and I wasn't to worry. She agreed that I should keep trying to get through to oncology, as appointments had probably crossed over. Like me, she didn't want me going for another CT scan and more radiation.

Tuesday 19 May 2015

I got my appointments sorted out. The CT scan was an overlap, a problem arising from being seen by two referring doctors at the same time. The wait for appointments is a crazy time for me, so no appointments tomorrow!

The Professor's secretary phoned and I am going to Liverpool for my appointment next Thursday 28th May, which if I'm honest I'll be relieved to have. The flights are booked. I can now let Lauren and the boys know about my tests. I'll try to chase my thoughts away with a little singing practice to get a few songs ready for another family do – this time for my niece's engagement on Saturday night.

Wednesday 20 May 2015

The appointment for my follow-up scan came in today. Unfortunately it's for the 28th when I will be in Liverpool. So I've had to phone and get a new date, and with my other appointment on the 3rd June it will have to be after that.

Thursday 21 May 2015

I finally got the results from the CT scan on the 12th May! They are reassured that my kidney did not show any lump. I'm being sent for a renogram to discover the reason for the blockage in the pole of my right kidney. As the letter says, this is certainly good news!

Sunday 24 May 2015

I received a phone call today from Q Radio asking if I would come along and sing at an event in Ballymoney on 6th June. I panicked for a moment, then said yes! I panicked because the night before I sang at my niece's engagement party I had been a little nervous. So I had decided that I would just settle myself until I was in a better place. I didn't need to be putting myself under this pressure, plus the timing was bad with me having a test on the 3rd. But I really wanted to do it; I needed to be brave. I was afraid of losing my nerve. I had worked so hard to build my confidence and I could feel it slipping away, so I needed to do it for me.

Back in November I had been asked to sing in the music department of Cameron's Department Store in Ballymena. It was a great boost for my confidence and the first time I had sung without the pressure of organising it. I was just there, singing. People came and went, stopped and listened. Some even sang along. I loved it.

Wednesday 26 May 2015

I got an email from Q Radio yesterday asking me to come in to the station to do a live interview. It would go out on three radio stations. They thought it would be good publicity for me. I hope it is progress for me, because I am more excited than I am nervous. Then today I got another email to say the event had to be rescheduled. I was glad I didn't stay awake worrying about it, but I was also relieved, thinking it might all have been too much because of my appointment that week. I'm sorted and ready for my appointment in Liverpool tomorrow. I hope it goes well.

Monday 1 June 2015

On a day that's miserable with wind and rain all I can do is lie here resting. You see, I had my appointment last Thursday in Liverpool. The Professor wasn't there for the first time since I have been going, so his colleague saw me. An early morning flight and taxi into the hospital got me there just after 9.30 a.m., in time for my appointment. I had my usual tests, then I went in to see the ophthalmologist. I have fluid in my eye, and after a look at my eye I was sent for another scan. The result showed that the macular had slightly detached. This is another side effect of the radiation treatment (radiation macular detachment). It may correct itself. If not, I'd have to have injections into my eye to save my sight. If the macular detached completely I'd go blind. Fluid in the eye is also a side effect. The tumour hasn't changed, but she says this is what she would expect at this early stage. Does this mean the radiation is still working? I forgot to ask, but it's the only thing that makes sense, as I'm still very aware of my eye and my eyelid still burns, making it very uncomfortable, especially when I wear make-up. She said she would document it all and show it to the Professor on Monday.

Saturday 6 June 2015

I'm very glad today that the date for the Q Radio event was changed. It will now be on Saturday 27th June. If it had been today I'd have failed to make the grade. My appointment on Wednesday for a hysteroscopy was not successful, so I'm being taken into hospital to go under general anaesthetic for the procedure. The doctor and nurses I met today were so kind to me. I can't express my thanks enough for getting me through another difficult day. I just wish I didn't have to go through it all again next week. Somehow life feels so hard to understand, as once again I cuddle my hot water bottle to help with the pain and emotion of the day.

Saturday 13 June 2015

One more test over this week. Last Wednesday I had the CT scan of my kidney. I was given a radiation injection and asked to lie completely still for thirty minutes. The lights were turned down and I heard a little Coldplay 'Fix you' – that was my song for Chrisy. He was with me at that moment. It reminded me that the very first day Chrisy had been for a scan in March 2007 I too had been having a scan in a different hospital.

I left for an hour and then returned for another five minute scan. I spent the rest of the day drinking and weeing, trying to flush the radiation out of my system so I'd be ready for my hospital procedure the next day.

Lauren arrived home in the early hours of Tuesday morning. She had driven all the way from Cork to take care of me after my procedure. She just needed to be here for me and I was so happy to see her. Lauren took me for the scan and to Whiteabbey Hospital for my 1 p.m. admission. I was all checked, gowned and ready to go when my urine sample came back showing a line. So a blood test had to be taken and a taxi called to deliver it to the lab in Antrim for testing. To keep everything right they had to be sure I wasn't pregnant. God blessed me with a great sense of humour, so all I could do was laugh and I am many times thankful for that. I explained how I'd had a test yesterday for a CT scan and it was okay. The doctor said that sometimes the tests show a false negative but because of the procedure they needed to be sure. The result was through just in time for my procedure slot – all clear. With no veins to show for myself (me, the master of good veins) I was taken into theatre and the anaesthetist prepared to knock me out. I was given a hysteroscopy and a polyp was removed and taken for biopsy. Why does hospital tea and toast taste so great? Could it be starvation or relief?

At 6.20 p.m. I was ready for home, thanks again to some very sweet nurses and the talents of doctors. I was handed over to Lauren's care for twenty-four hours, bless her.

For many years I was so flexible I didn't know who I was, and now that I'm discovering who I am, I think 'OK, I know where I stand on that issue. Now on to the next one.' But I have to remind myself that all issues are interrelated – no one is separate.

~ Kathleen Casey Theisen

Friday 24 July 2015

I went back to my doctor three weeks ago to see if they had got any results from my scan or biopsy. 'Yes, they're back and they're both clear. Do you think you could be stressed?' she asked me. I'm thinking: seriously, is that a question? I got a prescription to treat gastritis and was told to come back in a month if the pain hadn't gone away and not to worry! Worry! What did I possibly have to worry about, I thought to myself. I wanted to say: I need you to keep fighting with me. If I'm here it's because I need help. I'm not stressed today, though Lord knows I should be. Know me. Remember me. If you could even once ask me how I am and how I'm coping with my treatment. Allow me more than a ten-minute slot. I don't come to you thinking, oh, I have a pain; it must be cancer. I'm sure cancer patients suffer from other things.

I left feeling slightly disheartened, annoyed that after three weeks' wait no one had let me know my result, and that three months on I was still in pain. I am now being referred for an endoscopy (a camera down the throat into the stomach) to see if it shows up the cause of my stomach pain. Two days later I got an appointment to attend the Causeway Hospital and I thought, what's going on? My test was clear. I had to wait another three weeks to find out. Grrrr!!

Going to the hospital today I was a little curious about what he had to say, given that the last time I spoke to him he had said that if everything was okay he wouldn't be seeing me again, that I'd get the results through my doctor. But he had asked to see me, so I wondered what he had found.

It appears that my kidney is slightly larger on my right side and that I was born that way. It gave the impression that there was a mass or blockage, and as the nurses at oncology back in April had suspected, it showed up as a shadow. I think he just wanted to put my mind at rest and make sure I knew about it in case it showed up again in a later scan. He is now referring me for an MRI of my spine. He thinks it could be nerve damage – I was knocked down while walking through the shopping centre back in September 2014 and broke my coccyx (tailbone). He thinks my pain is coming from this. I was just three songs away from finishing the recording of my third album when I had the fall. So I finished it quite literally on the edge of my seat.

Sunday 2 August 2015

The best part of my life so far has been during the time when I was clear for a year. I found the bravest part of me through new friends. I learned to trust in myself to stand alone and make my way no matter what tried to hold me back. It is sometimes in your loneliness you discover a better version of yourself. Holding on to that is sometimes a struggle, but each new day brings hope.

Though we be sick and tired and faint and worn – Lo, all things can be borne!
~ Elizabeth Chase Akers

Epilogue

When I was first told I had a tumour in my eye I did that thing that everyone does and looked it up on the internet. I was horrified when I read the prognosis could be five years.

Heading into my fourth year of uncertainty and knowing that I have to be clear for three years, I'm getting through day by day … sure aren't we all

I am thankful for so much. In between the events recorded in my journal I have lived, laughed and surprised myself and others with my resilience, such as driving around Scotland, three Irish people and two crazy Americans, a trip I will treasure, along with other memorable trips; and nights of great music and friendships made. I have often wondered how my daughter, especially, coped. For us it has very much been a mother–daughter journey, building a relationship that will sustain us for a long time. It all came down to laughter, reminding ourselves to laugh and keep laughing. (Did you know people with cancer aren't supposed to laugh or look well? It always amazes me how others see the illness, not the person and their strength of character.)

I've had difficult times. It was only through keeping this journal that I could free myself of the daily thoughts and the sense of helplessness I felt as I struggled to get to a normal place. I constantly try to hold on to parts of the person I was, too afraid to let go in case I fall. Each time I get pulled back, I fall a little further. At first I'm weak, but then I return stronger, more determined to live for the future.

Now I barely know who I am. Now my family only see glimpses of who I was. Thank God they were grown enough to remember I was a great mum.

During the very difficult times, I went to that place of frantically sorting things out, things like the kids' school stuff, their toys, making sure they were all separated out; their memory boxes, for want of a better term, containing photos, my little books and scraps of paper that I hope one day will hold great memories for them. I panicked because, with the best of intentions, sometimes I needed to edit those words. Being a close family they will fill in the missing or edited parts. They lived every part of it with me, each in their own way.

So to that one professional who thought it a brave choice of words to say, on one of my visits after my first clear appointment back in 2012, 'It's all good. It's as if it had never happened', and then have to tell me a few months later that it had returned: it did happen, and it happened again and again. No one can ever prepare you for the C word, especially the first time you hear it. They need to remember that it's you they're telling, it's you they're talking about.

It took me almost a year to admit to myself that I had cancer. It wasn't that I didn't accept it, I just found it the hardest word to get out of my mouth. With help, when I finally said it out loud it was such a relief and released something in me so overwhelming that no words can really explain it. For a few days my body ached with the sheer relief of exposing myself to the idea that I wasn't going to allow it to control me. There, I had said it; I had said it out loud to someone else. It made me cry, but when the relief left my body I felt great.

On a visit to my doctor after my first treatment had been successful he asked me, 'What happens now?' I said that I didn't know; I supposed I'd just carry on with my life, given that my cancer is quite unusual. I didn't feel that I could talk about it. I'd always been told, 'Well you look good. You'd never know you had cancer.' (The perception is that cancer patients are thin and have lost their hair.) But the reality is we look every bit as normal as everyone else (Chrisy never looked like he had cancer until the chemotherapy kicked in). The other reality is that you are very much on your own; your family are very much on their own. You get through by telling yourself there are people worse off than you. Of course, this is always true, but it's of no consolation when you're going through the tough parts and holding yourself together for everyone around you. During those times you are all that matters.

I will be back in Liverpool in December 2015 to see how my treatment is working. For now I'm enjoying looking at life through both eyes. If the time comes when I do lose the sight in my left eye, I will keep living the best life I can, and draw strength from my journey and my singing. For me, it's about knowing it, then accepting it.

As a cancer patient, I don't want to hear, 'Oh it must have been something you ate … something you drank … something you drank out off … my curtains … the air.' Give me a break! I have to get through what I suffer as a cancer patient without carrying around a load of guilt as well. Be a friend. You know me best. Let's just eat cake … and have a good old laugh! Laughing is my favourite!

The secret of seeing is to sail on solar wind. Hone and spread your spirit, till you yourself are a sail, whetted, translucent, broadside to the merest puff.
~ Annie Dillard

About the author

I have tests in the Oncology Unit in Belfast City Hospital and in the eye clinic at The Royal Liverpool Hospital, and sometimes in The Royal Victoria Hospital, Belfast, every six months for the foreseeable future. Knowing that I have been able to help others through this book and my singing makes me incredibly happy. 'There but for the grace of God.'

I should have known I would have been strong enough. I left home at the age of eighteen to join my boyfriend of three months, now my husband, in Australia. Then at the age of twenty and a few months after we married, we took on the world of work from our kitchen table (my office) and set up a plumbing business together, later turning it into a private house building business. In our mid thirties we returned to our roots when we bought a farm. One of the hardest things for me recently has been my inability to help out on the farm; I miss it very much. I still have my secretarial work, and for that I am very thankful, and now I also sing. I have also written a few songs. I am very much looking forward to one day having music put to my words and recording them.

Cancer scared the life out of me, but surprisingly, it also scared the life *into* me. I am so glad that through this I faced my biggest fear – singing in front of people. The thought that everyone's eyes would be on me as I stood in front of them to sing was my fear. The stark reality that I could possibly lose my sight gave me the push to just do it, to at least give it a go. From a very early age I have enjoyed singing – I've been told I sang in my playpen. My dad wanted me to be called Kathleen, because he knew a girl called Kathleen who was a great singer and he wanted me to be a singer. It all feels very surreal. I used to listen to Big T (Trevor Campbell) on Downtown Radio when I was growing up, and now he is playing my music.

After sending my last album to Trevor, he emailed me to thank me for reminding him of a song he had forgotten about ('Just About Now' by Faith Hill). This was a song I had sung around the house, and my children grew up listening to it. When I had my fall back in September I had to change the song I was originally going to record because it was a fast song and I was in so much pain. So I chose 'Just About Now' instead and did it in one take. Now Big T was talking about it on the radio and saying how much he loved it. It is an email I will treasure, that and the one I received from Adrian Dempsey, also at Downtown Radio, who encouraged me with my music. It's times like this I am so glad I faced my fear. I am thankful to Big T and Downtown Radio for bringing my music to people who would otherwise not know of me. Sometimes I get the nicest messages from people thanking me for sharing my voice with them. I've had messages from as far away as America and Canada.

The fact that our families were so shocked that I could sing made it all the more special when, for the first time, I stood out in front of them and sang on 24th October 2013.

The idea has gained currency that woman have been handicapped not only by fear of failure – not unknown to men either – but by fear of success as well.
~ Sonya Rudikoff

Katie's music

Massive thanks to all who have purchased my albums. I have been humbled by your generosity. Proceeds from CD sales is going to The Christopher McKeown Memorial Fund.

The main aim of the fund is to help children and young adults whose lives have been affected by cancer. A donation from the fund will go towards something for the recipient. This can be unrelated to their treatment. Televisions, PlayStations and games, plus two tablets have been donated to the Belfast City Hospital Cancer Centre and Young Adult services. We are very grateful to everyone who makes donations to the fund so we can help bring a little light into their lives.

Chrisy asked his family to set up a charity in his name. He had raised a lot of money over the years of his illness and wanted them to continue to help others affected by cancer.

My music is available for purchase on my website: www.katiemckay.co.uk where you can also find a link to my Facebook page.

It Gets Better (October 2013)
'Adam's Song' (single) (February 2014)
I'm Alright (May 2014)
The Girl I Am (October 2014)

YouTube video of 'I Know a Heartache' (from my first album) released 13th May 2014
https://www.youtube.com/watch?v=Ff2NdsLYX5Y

Acknowledgements

Katie and her daughter Lauren present a cheque for £1,455 to staff at The Royal Liverpool Eye Clinic. The money was raised at their Blue Eyes benefit night in August 2012.
Left to right: Dr Angi, Lauren McKay, Katie McKay, Mrs Laura Edmunds.

My heartfelt thanks go to: the NHS; The Mater Eye Clinic; The Royal Liverpool Eye Clinic; The Royal Victoria Eye Clinic; Belfast City Hospital Oncology Unit; Clatterbridge Oncology Hospital in the Wirral; and Patient Care who organise my flights and help with expenses.

To Kathy Delargy, my optician at Eye Connection: thanks will never be enough for always being there for me and caring.

To the Professors at The Royal Liverpool Eye Clinic at St Paul's; to all the ophthalmologists, especially Miss McAvoy at The Royal Victoria Eye Clinic/Mater Eye Clinic, who have been with me from the start; to my doctors and all the doctors and nurses at the many hospital appointments I've attended. To date, I have had just over fifty appointments. You are an incredible bunch of people. I am many times thankful to those who showed me their heart.

My thanks to author Bernie McGill for her encouragement and support.

Thanks also to Lelia, Karen and David who didn't know me at the start of this book. They made a lot of things possible and became my friends.

Finally, to my family, friends and wider family circle, thanks for your love, tears, prayer's and support.

> *A day of worry is more exhausting than a week of work.*
> ~ John Lubbock

Thank you, Karen Casey, for allowing me to use some of the quotes from your book, *Each Day a New Beginning: Daily Meditations for Women*. I highly recommend it. Karen's words really lifted me. If you get the chance to read it yourself you will understand.

When I let Lauren read through this journal she said, 'You haven't shown enough of your funny side.' But the thing was, I didn't need to write when I was happy. I needed to write when I needed to talk. At the start I never expected to write a book. It was just a release of my thoughts and fears – a way of letting it go.

In my eye a seed was planted. That seed made me grow. In my loneliness I grew to sing, to write music, to write this book, to face my fears. Tears are rain for the soul; keep your soul peaceful.

Daydreaming is also good for the soul!

> *Proceeds from the sale of this book will go to*
> *The Royal Liverpool Eye Clinic*

Love you, Mum …
Thank you for making me.

Made in the USA
Columbia, SC
18 July 2017